This book of memory verses
BELONGS TO

I have hidden your word in my heart, that I might not sin against you.
Psalm 119:11 NLT
(New Living Translation)

I will put my heart to study His word.

colour me

Study to shew thyself approved unto God, a workman that needeth not to be ashamed, rightly dividing the word of truth.
2 Timothy 2:15 KJV

I will listen when I am taught His word.

colour me

Study this Book of Instruction continually. Meditate on it day and night so you will be sure to obey everything written in it. Only then will you prosper and succeed in all you do.

Joshua 1:8 NLT

Genesis

"In the beginning, God created the heavens and the earth.
Genesis 1:1

Just as this passage reads, dear Lord in everything I do help me be creative.

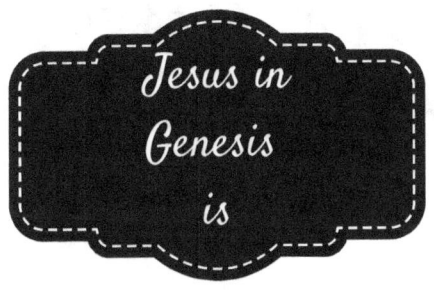

Our Creator

Exodus

"If it is true that you look favourably on me, let me know your ways so I may understand you more fully and continue to enjoy your favour. And remember that this nation is your very own people."
Exodus 33:13 NLT

Just as this passage reads, dear Lord I want to know your ways and understand you fully. I also like to enjoy your favour everyday of my life.

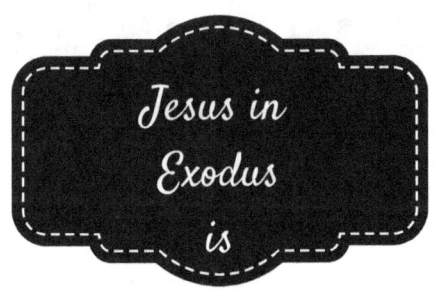

The Passover Lamb

Leviticus

"So do not act like the people in Egypt, where you used to live, or like the people of Canaan, where I am taking you. You must not imitate their way of life."
Leviticus 18:3 NLT

Just as this passage reads, dear Lord help me act like you at all times and not like men who don't know or serve you.

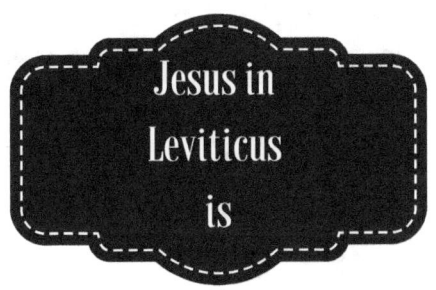

High Priest

Numbers

"God said.... "I speak to him face to face, clearly, and not in riddles! He sees the Lord as he is. So why were you not afraid to criticize my servant Moses?"
Numbers 12:8 NLT

Just as this passage reads, dear Lord help me hear you clearly, don't make me criticize your servant who you have called.

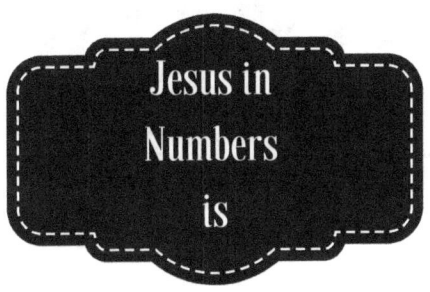

Water in the desert

Deuteronomy

"Remember the Lord your God. He is the one who gives you power to be successful, in order to fulfill the covenant he confirmed to your ancestors with an oath."
Deuteronomy 8:18 NLT

Just as this passage reads, dear Lord thank you for giving me power to be successful.

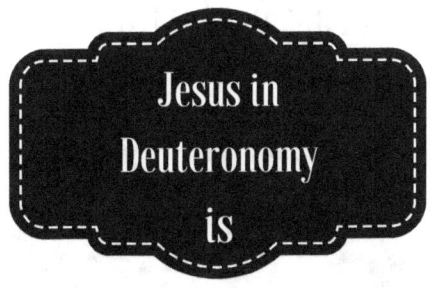

Our Eagles wings of Deliverance

Joshua

"This is my command—be strong and courageous! Do not be afraid or discouraged. For the Lord your God is with you wherever you go."
Joshua 1:9 NLT

Just as this passage reads, dear Lord in all that I do, let me know you are with me wherever I go. Help me be strong and courageous.

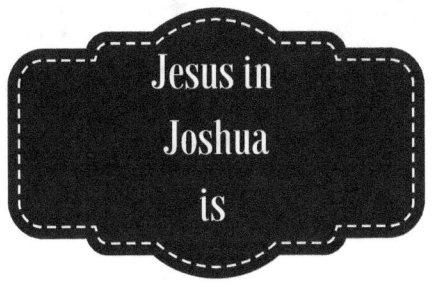

Commander of the army of the Lord

Judges

"And the Spirit of the Lord began to stir him while he lived in Mahaneh-dan, which is located between the towns of Zorah and Eshtaol."
Judges 13:25 NLT

Just as this passage reads, dear Lord let the Holy Spirit continue to stir me in the way I should go.

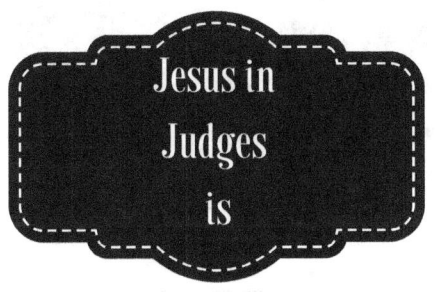

The Perfect Judge

Ruth

"Then Naomi said to her, "Just be patient, my daughter, until we hear what happens. The man won't rest until he has settled things today."
Ruth 3:18 NLT

Just as this passage reads, dear Lord, let me be patient while I await my goodness.

The Kinsman Redeemer

1 Samuel

"But Samuel, though he was only a boy, served the Lord. He wore a linen garment like that of a priest."
1 Samuel 2:18 NLT

Just as this passage reads, dear Lord, help me serve you like Samuel did as a little child.

The Prophet, Priest and King

2 Samuel

"But in my distress I cried out to the Lord; yes, I cried to my God for help. He heard me from his sanctuary; my cry reached his ears."
2 Samuel 22:7 NLT

Just as this passage reads, dear Lord hear me from your sanctuary when I cry to you for help.

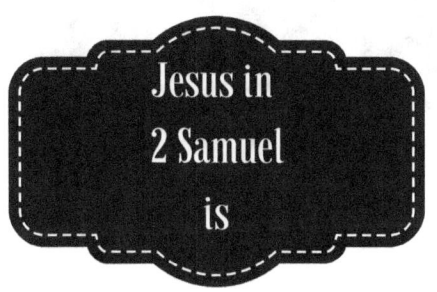

True son of David

1 Kings

"God gave Solomon very great wisdom and understanding, and knowledge as vast as the sands of the seashore."
1 Kings 4:29 NLT

Just as this passage reads, dear Lord give me great wisdom, understanding and knowledge like you gave Solomon.

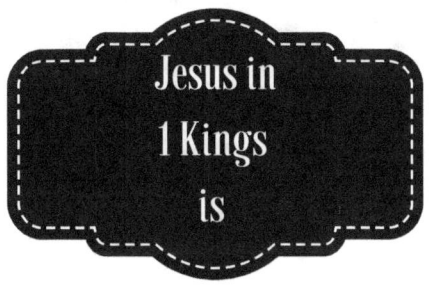

The Promise Keeper

2 Kings

"Now, O Lord our God, rescue us from his power; then all the kingdoms of the earth will know that you alone, O Lord, are God."
2 Kings 19:19 NLT

Just as this passage reads, dear Lord in everything I do help me be creative.

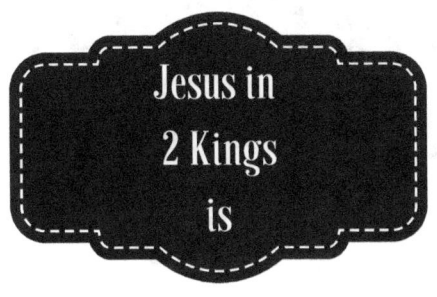

The Jealous God

1 Chronicles

"He was the one who prayed to the God of Israel, "Oh, that you would bless me and expand my territory! Please be with me in all that I do, and keep me from all trouble and pain!" And God granted him his request."
1 Chronicles 4:10 NLT

_____

_____

_____

_____

_____

Just as this passage reads, dear Lord grant me all that I request for, bless and keep me from all trouble.

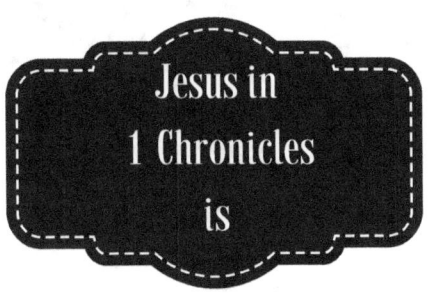

He's our Reigning King

2 Chronicles

"I am sending you a master craftsman named Huram-abi, who is extremely talented."
2 Chronicles 2:13 NLT

Just as this passage reads, dear Lord make me extremely talented, let men refer my work/arts for others to see and use.

The Deliverer

Ezra

"This was because Ezra had determined to study and obey the Law of the Lord and to teach those decrees and regulations to the people of Israel."
Ezra 7:10 NLT

Just as this passage reads, dear Lord help me be determined in studying my book and your word. Let me obey all that is in it.

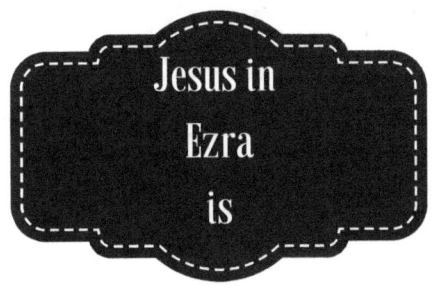

The Faithful Scribe

Do you know any singer in the bible?

colour me

Do you know any carpenter in the bible?

colour me

Nehemiah

"They were just trying to intimidate us, imagining that they could discourage us and stop the work. So I continued the work with even greater determination."
Nehemiah 6:9 NLT

Just as this passage reads, dear Lord don't let me get discouraged or intimidated by others in doing that which you have asked I do. Help me stay focus and continue in your work.

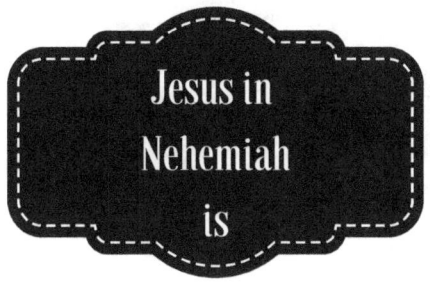

The Rebuilder of Broken Walls

Esther

"Mordecai the Jew became the prime minister, ... He was very great among the Jews, ... because he continued to work for the good of his people and to speak up for the welfare of all their descendants."
Esther 10:3 NLT

Just as this passage reads, dear Lord help me work for the good of others and speak up for their welfare.

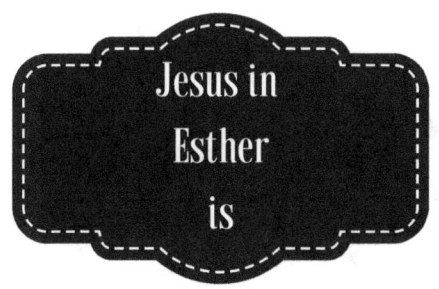

Protector

Job

"Even a tree has more hope! If it is cut down, it will sprout again and grow new branches."
Job 14:7 NLT

Just as this passage reads, dear Lord let me continue to hope in you, knowing in you I have peace.

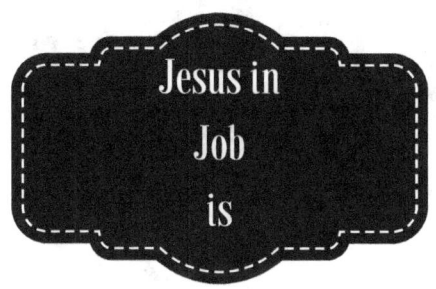

Mediator between God and Man

Psalms

"Yes, I have more insight than my teachers, for I am always thinking of your laws."
Psalms 119:99 NLT

Just as this passage reads, dear Lord let me continue to think about your word so I have more understanding than my teachers.

My Lord who is my Shepherd

Proverbs

"Trust in the Lord with all your heart; do not depend on your own understanding."
Proverbs 3:5 NLT

Just as this passage reads, dear Lord help me trust in you with all my heart, let me not depend on my understanding.

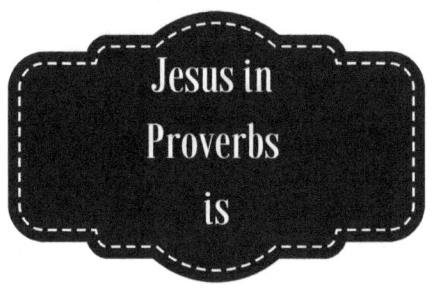

Our Wisdom

Ecclesiastes

"For everything there is a season, a time for every activity under heaven."
Ecclesiastes 3:1 NLT

Just as this passage reads, dear Lord help me know the season I am in so I know what activity is expected of me.

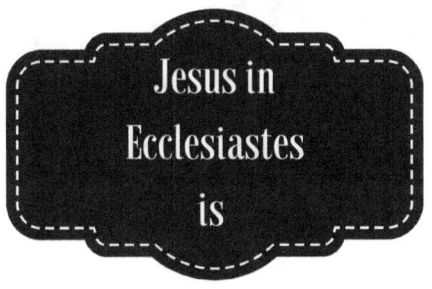

Our True Satisfaction

Songs of Songs

"Many waters cannot quench love, nor can rivers drown it. If a man tried to buy love with all his wealth, his offer would be utterly scorned."
Song of Songs 8:7 NLT

Just as this passage reads, dear Lord teach me to love genuinely, let my love for you be unquenchable. Let me not try to buy love for any reason.

The Beautiful Bridegroom

Isaiah

"Arise, Jerusalem! Let your light shine for all to see. For the glory of the Lord rises to shine on you."
Isaiah 60:1 NLT

Just as this passage reads, dear Lord thank you for your glory shining on me. Strengthen me to arise so the light you shine on me shall be seen by all.

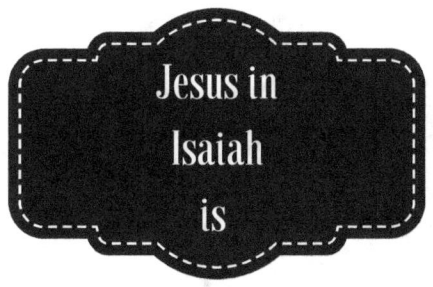

The Suffering Servant

Jeremiah

"If you look for me wholeheartedly, you will find me."
Jeremiah 29:13 NLT

Just as this passage reads, dear Lord let me long and thirsty after you with my whole heart, make me find you when I look for you.

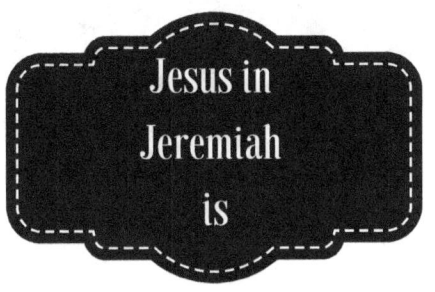

The Righteous Branch

Lamentations

"Who can command things to happen without the Lord's permission?"
Lamentations 3:37 NLT

Just as this passage reads, dear Lord thank you for having the last say and granting permission before anything happens to me.

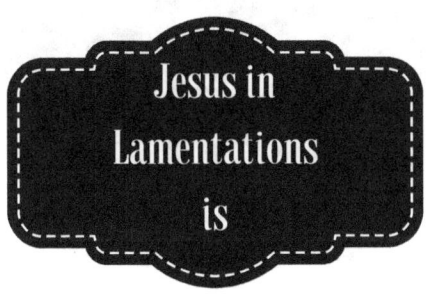

The Weeping Prophet

Ezekiel

"I will make my home among them. I will be their God, and they will be my people."
Ezekiel 37:27 NLT

Just as this passage reads, dear Lord continue to make my life your home.

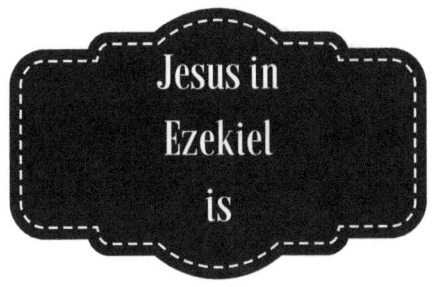

The Son of Man

Daniel

"I thank and praise you, God of my ancestors, for you have given me wisdom and strength. You have told me what we asked of you and revealed to us what the king demanded."
Daniel 2:23 NLT

Just as this passage reads, dear Lord thank you for giving me wisdom, strength and revealing all that seem difficult to me.

The Fourth Man in the Furnace

Hosea

"O Israel, stay away from idols! I am the one who answers your prayers and cares for you. I am like a tree that is always green; all your fruit comes from me."

Hosea 14:8 NLT

Just as this passage reads, dear Lord thank you for answering my prayers and caring for me.

The Faithful Husband

Joel

"Once again you will have all the food you want, and you will praise the Lord your God, who does these miracles for you. Never again will my people be disgraced."
Joel 2:26 NLT

_____

_____

_____

_____

_____

Just as this passage reads, dear Lord thank you for providing all the food I want, I praise you for these miracles.

The One who Restores

Amos

"I will firmly plant them there in their own land. They will never again be uprooted from the land I have given them," says the Lord your God."
Amos 9:15 NLT

Just as this passage reads, dear Lord thank you for planting me firmly in the land you have given me.

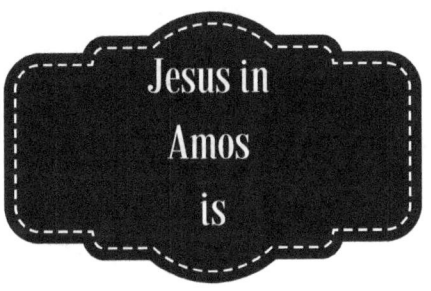

The Burden Bearer

Do you know anyone who played an instrument?

colour me

Do you know anyone who devised artistic designs in the bible?

colour me

Obadiah

"Because of the violence you did to your close relatives in Israel, you will be filled with shame and destroyed forever."
Obadiah 1:10 NLT

Just as this passage reads, dear Lord let me be considerate of my close relatives and not meet violence on them.

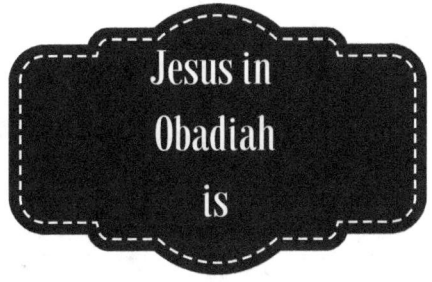

The Mighty Judge

Jonah

"But I will offer sacrifices to you with songs of praise, and I will fulfill all my vows. For my salvation comes from the Lord alone."
Jonah 2:9 NLT

Just as this passage reads, dear Lord my salvation comes from you and I offer my praise back to you.

The Foreign Missonary

Micah

"No, O people, the Lord has told you what is good, and this is what he requires of you: to do what is right, to love mercy, and to walk humbly with your God."
Micah 6:8 NLT

Just as this passage reads, dear Lord help me do what is right, to love mercy and walk humbly before you.

Our Peace

Nahum

"The Lord is good, a strong refuge when trouble comes. He is close to those who trust in him."
Nahum 1:7 NLT

Just as this passage reads, dear Lord thank you for being close to me and keeping me safe in times of trouble.

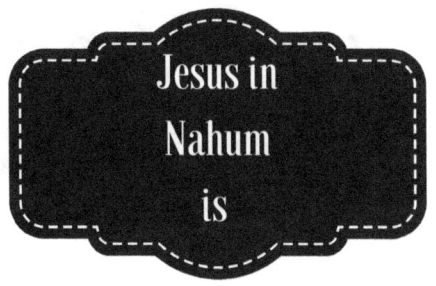

The Avenger

Habakkuk

"Then the Lord said to me, "Write my answer plainly on tablets, so that a runner can carry the correct message to others."
Habakkuk 2:2 NLT

_____

_____

_____

_____

_____

Just as this passage reads, dear Lord teach me to right the answers you give me so I can give the correct response to those who need it.

The Lord in His Holy Temple

Zephaniah

"For the Lord your God is living among you. He is a mighty savior. He will take delight in you with gladness. With his love, he will calm all your fears. He will rejoice over you with joyful songs."
Zephaniah 3:17 NLT

Just as this passage reads, dear Lord, my mighty saviour, thank you for taking delight in me with gladness.

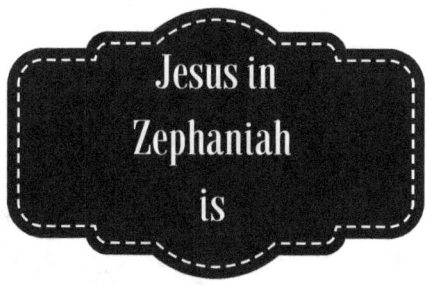

The Lord Mighty to Save

Haggai

"My Spirit remains among you, just as I promised when you came out of Egypt. So do not be afraid."
Haggai 2:5 NLT

Just as this passage reads, dear Lord let your Spirit remain with me as you promised and help me not be afraid.

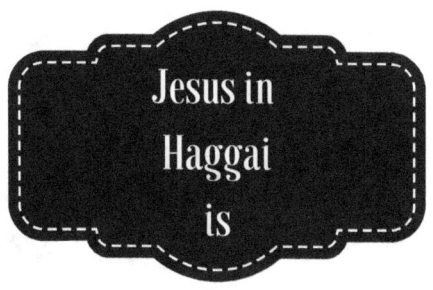

The Lord of Hosts

Zechariah

"By my power I will make my people strong, and by my authority they will go wherever they wish. I, the Lord, have spoken!"
Zechariah 10:12 NLT

_____

_____

_____

_____

_____

Just as this passage reads, dear Lord let your power continue to make me strong, and your authority make me go wherever I wish to go.

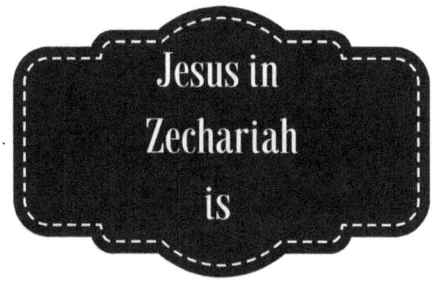

The Fountain of Cleansing

MALACHI

"I am the Lord, and I do not change. That is why you descendants of Jacob are not already destroyed."
Malachi 3:6 NLT

Just as this passage reads, dear Lord thank you for being my Lord who never change.

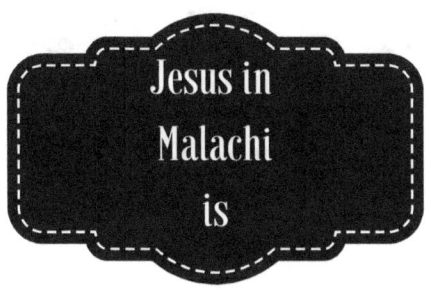

The Sun of Righteousness

MATHEW

"Do to others whatever you would like them to do to you. This is the essence of all that is taught in the law and the prophets."
Matthew 7:12 NLT

Just as this passage reads, dear Lord help me do to others what I would like them to do to me.

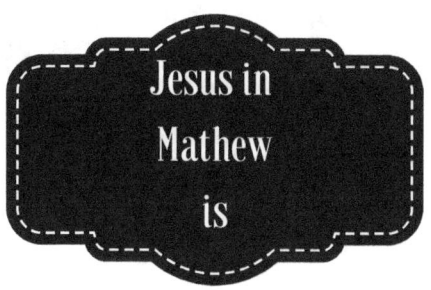

The Promised Messiah

MARK

"Jesus looked at them intently and said, "Humanly speaking, it is impossible. But not with God. Everything is possible with God."
Mark 10:27 NLT

Just as this passage reads, dear Lord I am thankful because with you all things are possible.

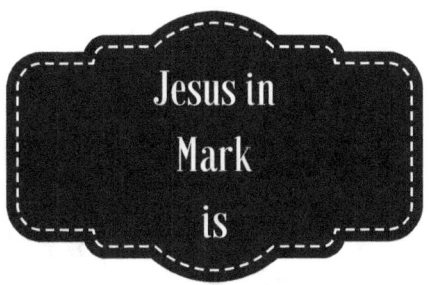

The Faithful Servant

LUKE

"Do not judge others, and you will not be judged. Do not condemn others, or it will all come back against you. Forgive others, and you will be forgiven."
Luke 6:37 NLT

Just as this passage reads, dear Lord help me learn to forgive others and not judge or condemn them.

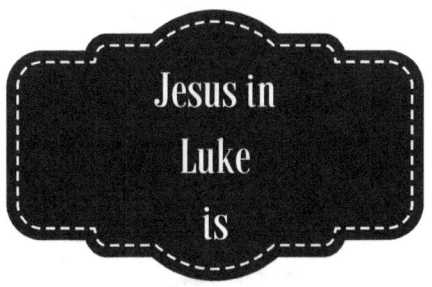

Friend of Sinners

JOHN

" "Don't let your hearts be troubled. Trust in God, and trust also in me."
John 14:1 NLT

Just as this passage reads, dear Lord let my trust continuously be in you, so I have no reason to be worried.

The Son of God

ACTS OF APOSTLES

"But Peter and the apostles replied, "We must obey God rather than any human authority."
Acts of the Apostles 5:29 NLT

Just as this passage reads, dear Lord teach me to obey you at all times.

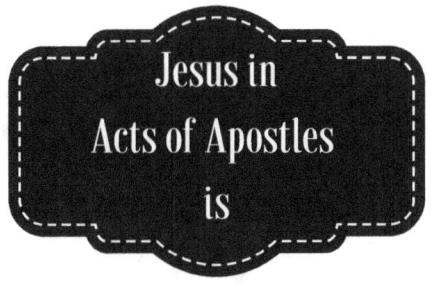

The Ascended Lord

ROMANS

"Don't copy the behavior and customs of this world, but let God transform you into a new person by changing the way you think. Then you will learn to know God's will for you, which is good and pleasing and perfect."
Romans 12:2 NLT

Just as this passage reads, dear Lord change the way I think and transform me into what you want me to be. Help me not copy the ways of the world.

The Justifier

Who in the bible was happy to tell others about God?

Colour .

Who sat at the feet of Jesus to listen as he spoke?

colour .

1 CORINTHIANS

"But you must be careful so that your freedom does not cause others with a weaker conscience to stumble."
1 Corinthians 8:9 NLT

Just as this passage reads, dear Lord don't let the way I live cause others to sin.

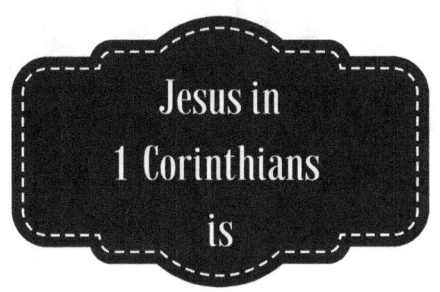

Our Righteousness

2 CORINTHIANS

"So we are Christ's ambassadors; God is making his appeal through us. We speak for Christ when we plead, "Come back to God!"
2 Corinthians 5:20 NLT

Just as this passage reads, dear Lord help me speak for you and make me a true ambassador of your kingdom.

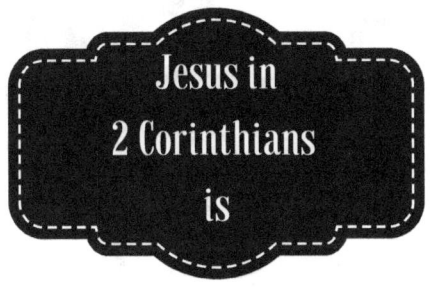

The God of all Comfort

GALATIANS

"So I say, let the Holy Spirit guide your lives. Then you won't be doing what your sinful nature craves."
Galatians 5:16 NLT

Just as this passage reads, dear Lord I ask that the Holy Spirit guide my life so I don't sin against thee.

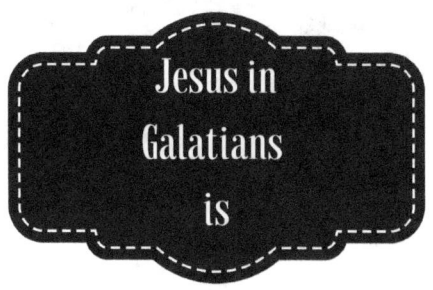

My Liberty

EPHESIANS

"Now all glory to God, who is able, through his mighty power at work within us, to accomplish infinitely more than we might ask or think."
Ephesians 3:20 NLT

Just as this passage reads, dear Lord I am grateful for the mighty power you gave me, that works in me to do all things especially my home working.

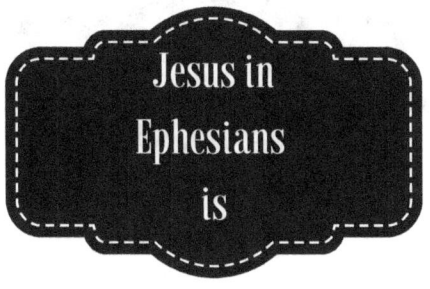

The Head of the Church

PHILIPPIANS

"Don't look out only for your own interests, but take an interest in others, too."
Philippians 2:4 NLT

Just as this passage reads, dear Lord teach me to look out for the interest of others as well as mine.

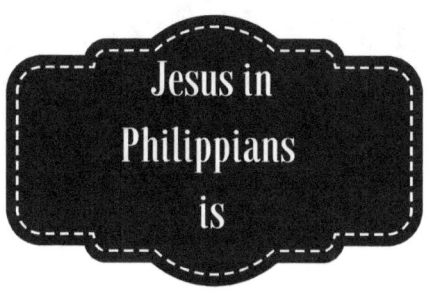

The All-Sufficient Christ

COLOSSIANS

"Put on your new nature, and be renewed as you learn to know your Creator and become like him."
Colossians 3:10 NLT

Just as this passage reads, dear Lord I want to be renewed daily so I can know you more and become like you.

The Fullness of God

1 THESSALONIANS

" "So encourage each other and build each other up, just as you are already doing."
1 Thessalonians 5:11 NLT

Just as this passage reads, dear Lord help me be there for others by encouraging them to do right.

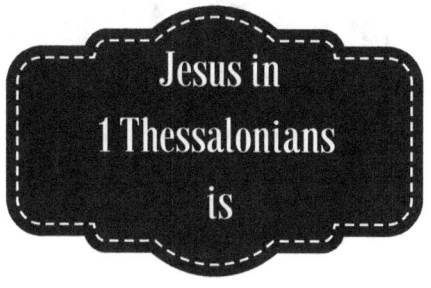

The Lord Coming Down from Heaven

2 THESSALONIANS

"So we keep on praying for you, asking our God to enable you to live a life worthy of his call. May he give you the power to accomplish all the good things your faith prompts you to do."
2 Thessalonians 1:11 NLT

Just as this passage reads, dear Lord help me remember to pray for others and give me the power to accomplish great things.

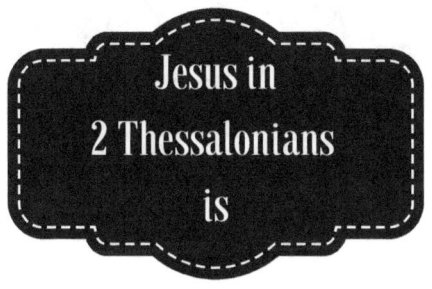

The Judge coming with Blazing Fire

1 TIMOTHY

"Don't let anyone think less of you because you are young. Be an example to all believers in what you say, in the way you live, in your love, your faith, and your purity."
1 Timothy 4:12 NLT

Just as this passage reads, dear Lord let what I say, the way I live, love and my faith in you be an example to all believers.

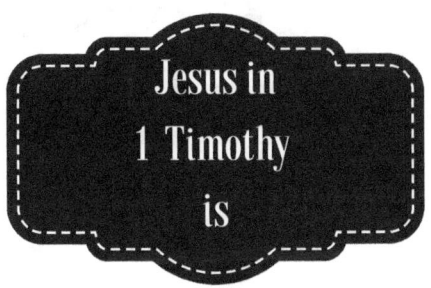

Our Mediator

2 TIMOTHY

"This is why I remind you to fan into flames the spiritual gift God gave you when I laid my hands on you."
2 Timothy 1:6 NLT

Just as this passage reads, dear Lord don't let the gifts you gave me be buried in me, show me how I can develop it for the good of all.

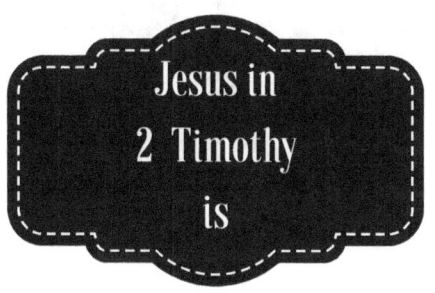

Our Master

TITUS

"Such people claim they know God, but they deny him by the way they live. They are detestable and disobedient, worthless for doing anything good."
Titus 1:16 NLT

Just as this passage reads, dear Lord I don't want the way I live to be different from the way you want me to live.

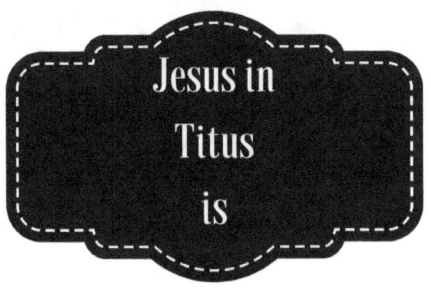

The Blessed Hope

PHILEMON

"Your love has given me much joy and comfort, my brother, for your kindness has often refreshed the hearts of God's people."
Philemon 1:7 NLT

Just as this passage reads, dear Lord let my love to others bring them joy, comfort and refreshing to their heart.

The one who paid our Debt

Do you know anyone in the bible who took a break from his role?

colour me

Do you know a dedicated solider in the bible?

colour me

HEBREWS

"Nothing in all creation is hidden from God. Everything is naked and exposed before his eyes, and he is the one to whom we are accountable."
Hebrews 4:13 NLT

Just as this passage reads, dear Lord I know nothing is hidden from you and I am accountable to you daily.

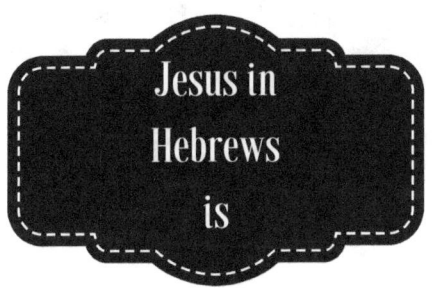

Our Great High Priest

JAMES

"If you need wisdom, ask our generous God, and he will give it to you. He will not rebuke you for asking."
James 1:5 NLT

_____

_____

_____

_____

_____

Just as this passage reads, dear Lord thank you for not rebuking me when I asked for wisdom. I lack wisdom, generous God please give me wisdom.

The Judge Standing at the Door

1 PETER

"But you are not like that, for you are a chosen people. You are royal priests, a holy nation, God's very own possession. As a result, you can show others the goodness of God, for he called you out of the darkness into his wonderful light."
1 Peter 2:9 NLT

Just as this passage reads, dear Lord thank you for choosing me, help me show others your goodness. Thank you Lord, for bringing me out of darkness into wonderful light.

The Chief Shepherd

2 PETER

"By his divine power, God has given us everything we need for living a godly life. We have received all of this by coming to know him, the one who called us to himself by means of his marvellous glory and excellence."

2 Peter 1:3 NLT

Just as this passage reads, dear Lord thank you for giving me everything I need to live a godly life. Thank you for your divine power working in me.

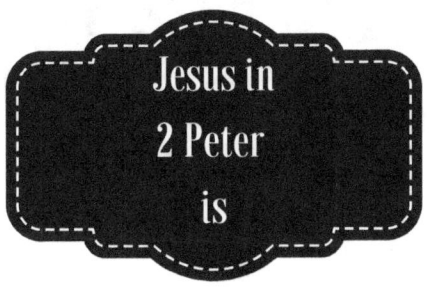

The Morning Star

1 JOHN

"If someone claims, "I know God," but doesn't obey God's commandments, that person is a liar and is not living in the truth."
1 John 2:4 NLT

Just as this passage reads, dear Lord help me live in truth by obeying your commandments.

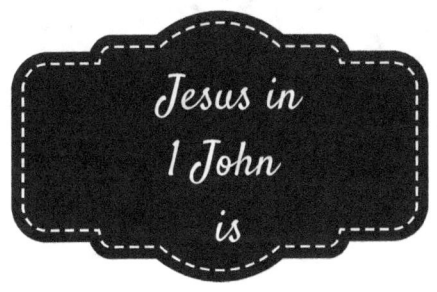

The Word of Life

2 JOHN

"If anyone comes to your meeting and does not teach the truth about Christ, don't invite that person into your home or give any kind of encouragement."
2 John 1:10 NLT

Just as this passage reads, dear Lord don't let me invite friends who won't speak or teach your truth.

Son of the Father

3 JOHN

"Dear friend, I hope all is well with you and that you are as healthy in body as you are strong in spirit."
3 John 1:2 NLT

Just as this passage reads, dear Lord help me learn to check on my friends to know how they are doing physically and spiritually.

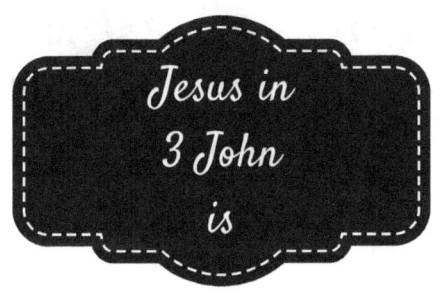

The Truth

JUDE

"But you, dear friends, must build each other up in your most holy faith, pray in the power of the Holy Spirit,"
Jude 1:20 NLT

Just as this passage reads, dear Lord I want to pray in the power of the Holy Spirit so I can build myself and friends up in our most holy faith.

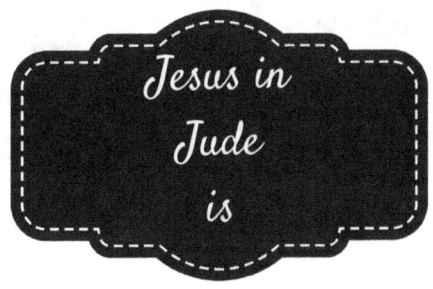

The Coming Lord with Countless Thousands of Saints

REVELATION

"I am the Alpha and the Omega—the beginning and the end," says the Lord God. "I am the one who is, who always was, and who is still to come—the Almighty One."
Revelation 1:8 NLT

Just as this passage reads, dear Lord thank you for being in the beginning and end of everything I do.
I love you Alpha and Omega.

The King of Kings and Lord of Lords

Now, I will go read my bible with my friend.

I will boldly tell others what I have learnt from His word.

www.ingramcontent.com/pod-product-compliance
Lightning Source LLC
Chambersburg PA
CBHW050029130526
44590CB00042B/2260